ABOUT THIS STUDY

Anything worth doing takes commitment. You know th that point comes where striving becomes strain. Then that key question moves menacingly into the foreground of your mind. Is it worth it? That's when the battle really begins. Are you in or are you out? In Paul's second letter to his spiritual protege, he plays the coach, but not the out-of-shape one yelling from the sidelines. He's finishing his own race and cheering Timothy on to push through the various obstacles that he will face. Paul's seen them all. And he's endured.

Even so, the message isn't one that has dark music playing in the background and a foreboding tone. It's more the musical score at the culmination of an intense battle scene or the overtime goal to win the world championship. It's sweat and blood dripping down over the lip past a big toothy grin in the close-up shot. It's worth it! Stick with it. Do what you've been trained to do. I'll be in that great cloud of witnesses going nuts when you cross that finish line. Don't get distracted or discouraged. The finish line is there and it's so good. That's also Christ's message to you this week. Endure!

ENDURANC

2 TIM 4:6-9

OnTrack Expedition: Endurance: 2 Timothy 4:6-9

Printed in the United States of America

Copyright © 2015 Pilgrimage Educational Resources

Any internet addresses, email addresses, phone numbers and physical addresses in this book are accurate at the time of publication. They are
provided as a resource. Pilgrimage Educational Resources does not endorse them or vouch for their content or permanence.

Author: Dwight E. Peterson
Executive Developer: Benjamin J. Wilhite
Graphic design by Lance Young (higherrockcreative.com)

ISBN-13 978-0692479315
ISBN 0692479317

10 9 8 7 6 5 4 3 2 1

2 TIM 4:1-9 (ESV)

1 I charge you in the presence of God and of Christ Jesus, who is to judge the living and the dead, and by his appearing and his kingdom: 2 preach the word; be ready in season and out of season; reprove, rebuke, and exhort, with complete patience and teaching. 3 For the time is coming when people will not endure sound teaching, but having itching ears they will accumulate for themselves teachers to suit their own passions, 4 and will turn away from listening to the truth and wander off into myths. 5 As for you, always be sober-minded, endure suffering, do the work of an evangelist, fulfill your ministry.

6 For I am already being poured out as a drink offering, and the time of my departure has come. 7 I have fought the good fight, I have finished the race, I have kept the faith. 8 Henceforth there is laid up for me the crown of righteousness, which the Lord, the righteous judge, will award to me on that Day, and not only to me but also to all who have loved his appearing.

PASSAGE
INTRO NOTES

Record key ideas from the passage introduction or from your first read through the entire passage. Write down any "big questions" on the tag below so you can revisit them during the week.

EXPEDITION

BIG questions this week...

1: SET GOALS

This exercise is designed to help prepare your heart and mind for the week of your upcoming event. Take some time to get alone and answer them. Good goals should be specific and measurable.

(1) Complete the following sentences to help you formulate some goals for the week:

This week, I hope I...

This week, I hope we as a group...

(2) Complete the following sentences to help you begin to formulate a strategy for seeing the above goals fulfilled:

In light of my answers above, I must...

In light of my answers above, we must...

(3) Complete the following sentences to help you formulate a plan to avoid what will derail your goals:

In light of my answers, I must not...

In light of my answers, we must not...

2: PLAN & COMMIT

Take your responses from the previous questions and write out a "personal commitment" for the week. That is, what are you going to personally commit to be doing this week and commit to not be doing. You will sign it and seek out at least one other person on the trip who will read it, pray for its fulfillment, and keep you accountable to it. If possible, seek out a second witness that will not be part of the event group that will pray for you during the event and will check in with you afterward to see how it went.

I, _____, personally commit to

I further commit to not

Name: _____

Signature: _____

Witness #1: _____

Witness #2: _____

Date: ____ / ____ / ____

1ST DAY
THE END

1: JOURNAL

Experiences
What experiences have you faced in the last 24 hours?

Questions
What questions do you find yourself asking?

Conclusions
What kind of conclusions are you coming to about yourself and others?

2: READ 2 TIMOTHY
Read through the entire book and record any thoughts or questions which are generated from what you read. In addition, record how the content relates to what you are dealing with this week.

3: EVALUATE
Answer the questions below based on 2 Timothy 4:6.

How does what Paul says to Timothy in verse 1-5 impact what he says here in verse 6?

What does it mean to be "poured out like a drink offering?" How does that impact what he is asking of Timothy?

What does it mean "the time has come for my departure?" How does it impact what Paul is asking of Timothy?

In what ways might you find yourself in similar circumstances to what Paul is talking to Timothy about?

How does what you are likely to face this week help you more fully understand this text?

4: INTEGRATE
Spend some time on each of the following activities to get the most out of today's study.

Memorize 2 Tim 4:7-8

Pray
Spend some time praying for yourself and for others in your group.

Commit
In light of what you see in yourself so far, what personal commitment will you make for today? Write it down...

Today, I'm praying for...

I commit to...

2ND DAY
GOOD FIGHT

1: JOURNAL

Experiences
What experiences have you faced in the last 24 hours?

Questions
What questions do you find yourself asking?

Conclusions
What kind of conclusions are you coming to about yourself and others?

EXPEDITION

2: READ 2 TIMOTHY
Read through the entire book and record any thoughts or questions which are generated from what you read. In addition, record how the content relates to what you are dealing with this week.

3: EVALUATE
Answer the questions below based on 2 Timothy 4:7.

What does it mean to "fight a good fight?"

Why does Paul use this analogy for Timothy?

How does this analogy relate to your own Christian walk?

In what ways have your responses during this week demonstrated that you are or are not living with a similar commitment? Back home?

In what ways can you be more aware of it for the remainder of the week? Back home?

4: INTEGRATE
Spend some time on each of the following activities to get the most out of today's study.

Memorize 2 Tim 4:7-8

Pray
Spend some time praying for yourself and for others in your group.

Commit
In light of what you see in yourself so far, what personal commitment will you make for today? Write it down...

Today, I'm praying for...

I commit to...

1: JOURNAL

Experiences
What experiences have you faced in the last 24 hours?

Questions
What questions do you find yourself asking?

Conclusions
What kind of conclusions are you coming to about yourself and others?

2: READ 2 TIMOTHY

Read through the entire book and record any thoughts or questions which are generated from what you read. In addition, record how the content relates to what you are dealing with this week.

3: EVALUATE
Answer the questions below based on 2 Timothy 4:7.

What does it mean to "finish the race?"

Why does Paul use this analogy for Timothy?

How does this analogy relate to your own Christian walk?

In what ways have your responses during the week demonstrated that you are or are not living with a similar commitment? Back home?

In what ways can you be more aware of it for the remainder of the week? Back home?

4: INTEGRATE
Spend some time on each of the following activities to get the most out of today's study.

Memorize 2 Tim 4:7-8

Pray
Spend some time praying for yourself and for others in your group.

Commit
In light of what you see in yourself so far, what personal commitment will you make for today? Write it down...

Today, I'm praying for...

I commit to...

1: JOURNAL

Experiences
What experiences have you faced in the last 24 hours?

Questions
What questions do you find yourself asking?

Conclusions
What kind of conclusions are you coming to about yourself and others?

2: READ 2 TIMOTHY
Read through the entire book and record any thoughts or questions which are generated from what you read. In addition, record how the content relates to what you are dealing with this week.

3: EVALUATE

Answer the questions below based on 2 Timothy 4:7.

What does it mean to "keep the faith?"

Why does Paul use this analogy for Timothy?

How does this analogy relate to your own Christian walk?

In what ways have your responses during this week demonstrated that you are or are not living with a similar commitment? Back home?

In what ways can you be more aware of it for the remainder of the week? Back home?

4: INTEGRATE

Spend some time on each of the following activities to get the most out of today's study.

Memorize 2 Tim 4:7-8

Pray
Spend some time praying for yourself and for others in your group.

Commit
In light of what you see in yourself so far, what personal commitment will you make for today? Write it down...

Today, I'm praying for...

I commit to...

5TH DAY
THE CROWN

1: JOURNAL

Experiences
What experiences have you faced in the last 24 hours?

Questions
What questions do you find yourself asking?

Conclusions
What kind of conclusions are you coming to about yourself and others?

2: READ 2 TIMOTHY
Read through the entire book and record any thoughts or questions which are generated from what you read. In addition, record how the content relates to what you are dealing with this week.

3: EVALUATE
Answer the questions below based on 2 Timothy 4:8.

What do you think the crown of righteousness is?

Why is this crown something which motivates us to daily have the kind of attitude we have been pursuing all week?

How does the fact that it is the Lord who will present it to you impact the significance of it?

How can this motivate you to achieve what Paul talks about in these verses when you get back to "real life?"

4: INTEGRATE
Spend some time on each of the following activities to get the most out of today's study.

Memorize 2 Tim 4:7-8

Pray
Spend some time praying for yourself and for others in your group.

Commit
In light of what you see in yourself so far, what personal commitment will you make for today? Write it down...

Today, I'm praying for...

I commit to...

1: EVALUATE

This exercise is designed to help discover and record the key takeaways from the week. Take some time to work through the process so you will get the most out of it.

(1) Take some time to read back through the pre trip contract you signed at the beginning of the week.

Write down some of the occasions where you fulfilled your commitment this week.

Write down some of the occasions where you struggled with your commitment this week.

List some of the experiences God used this week to challenge you in light of your commitment.

(2) Read back through your daily journal entries and Bible study notes and answer the questions below.

What opportunities did you have this week to be "poured out" or to endure hard things? How did you respond in those moments?

What opportunities did you have this week to "fight the good fight?" How did you respond in those moments?

How well did you "finish the race" this week? Be specific. What will it take to endure as you transition back to the "race of real life" after this week?

In what ways was your faith challenged this week? How did you respond in those moments, both in your heart of hearts and in your actions?

Paul talks about a crown of righteousness at the end of the race. What rewards or blessings did God give you and your group this week?

On the scale of 1 to 10 below, how well did you run your race this week? How well did your group run its race together? Circle one number for each line.

Me   1 2 3 4 5 6 7 8 9 10

The Group   1 2 3 4 5 6 7 8 9 10

2: APPLY

This exercise is designed to help connect your key takeaways to "real life" at home. Take some time to work through each of the steps below.

(1) Take a minute and think about what things will be like when you get home. Write down your thoughts.

What are you most looking forward to?

What are you least looking forward to?

(2) Where do you think it'll be most difficult to live out what you've learned?

(3) Where do you think it will be easiest to live out what you've learned?

3: COMMIT

Take your responses from the previous questions and write out a "personal commitment" for your transition to "real life." That is, what are you going to personally commit to be doing and commit to not be doing at home. You will sign it and seek out at least one other person from the trip who will read it, pray for its fulfillment, and keep you accountable to it. Also seek out a key person at home to share your commitment(s) with that will encourage you, pray for you and hold you accountable.

I, _____, personally commit to

I further commit to not

Name: _____

Signature: _____

Witness#1: _____

Witness#2: _____

Date: ____/____/____

MEET THE AUTHOR

Since 1985, Dwight Peterson has been an integral part of the mission and ministry of Pilgrimage Educational Resources. After serving for three years as Youth Pastor at Brookdale Baptist Church (Bloomfield, NJ), Dwight accepted the Youth Pastor role at First Baptist Church (Elkhart, IN), where he served for 14 years. His area of responsibility included junior high, senior high and college ministry along with oversight of the Bible curriculum and discipleship functions at the Christian school operated by the church. In Elkhart, Dwight developed training courses for his youth ministry teams while also making them available in workshop and written formats as curriculum to other youth ministries. Out of this, he created and has continuously developed OnTrack Devotions.

Currently, Mr. Peterson serves on the faculty of Summit University (Clarks Summit, PA) as well as carrying various responsibilities at PER. Dwight's goal at BBC, with Pilgrimage, or in everyday life is to disciple students. Whether that be in his Youth Ministry classes, leading a wilderness trip, coaching, or hanging out with the guys in the dorm, where he serves as Resident Director, growth is the end goal. For the past several years, Dwight has also been directing the TLC Youth Workers Conference.

Dwight Peterson

Role: Wilderness Institute Director

Where: Pilgrimage Educational Resources

Family: Married w/4 children and 6 grandchildren

Online: OnTrackDevotions.com

EDITION

WANT TO GROW SELF-FEEDERS?

EQUIP THEM... WITH A DEVOTIONAL TOOL THAT WORKS.

ONTRACK IS A DEVOTIONAL TOOL DESIGNED TO BUILD THE SKILL AND DISCIPLINE OF EFFECTIVE DAILY BIBLE STUDY FOR STUDENTS AND ADULTS. ITS UNIQUE APPROACH MODELS INDUCTIVE BIBLE STUDY METHODS AND ADDS VALUE FOR SMALL GROUP ACCOUNTABILITY THROUGH MONTHLY COMMITMENTS. OTD WALKS THE USER THROUGH A PROCESS OF DISCOVERY, UNLOCKING THE WORD BY TRAINING THEM HOW TO ASK GOOD QUESTIONS THROUGH REPETITION AND MODELING. TIME IN THE WORD BECOMES A REAL CONVERSATION WITH GOD. AVAILABLE IN DIGITAL AND PRINT EDITIONS.

PRINT EDITION
*3 SEASONAL VOLUMES PER YEAR
*PACES WITH MINISTRY SEASONS
*AS LOW AS $1.67 PER PERSON/MO

DIGITAL EDITION

DIGITAL EDITION
*MONTHLY PDF DOWNLOADS
*PRINTABLE IN BOOKLET FORM
*LICENSE FOR ENTIRE CHURCH LOCATION
*AS LOW AS $20.75/MO
 (ANNUAL SUBSCRIPTION)

WHAT MINISTRY LEADERS ARE SAYING...

WE'RE BIG FANS OF ONTRACK DEVOTIONS. IT'S SOLID, RELEVANT CONTENT THAT CHALLENGES TEENAGERS TO EMBRACE THE LIFE OF A CHRIST-FOLLOWER.

LES BRADFORD
YM360.COM

THERE IS NOTHING QUITE LIKE IT. I USE OTD DAILY AND WE USE IT IN OUR MINISTRIES SUCH AS URBAN HOPE (INNER CITY MINISTRY) AND MOMENTUM (YOUTH CONFERENCE).

ED LEWIS
BUILDMOMENTUM.ORG

PILGRIMAGE

PILGRIMAGE EDUCATIONAL RESOURCES / CLARKS SUMMIT, PA
P: 570.504.1463 / E: INFO@SIMPLYAPILGRIM.COM / SIMPLYAPILGRIM.COM

THE ONTRACK DEVOTIONS MILITARY EDITION IS A 12-MONTH STUDY THROUGH THE NEW TESTAMENT AND PROVERBS WRITTEN FOR TODAY'S MILITARY PERSONNEL. THE INCLUDED USER GUIDE WALKS THE READER THROUGH THE BASIC STEPS OF INDUCTIVE BIBLE STUDY (OBSERVATION, INTERPRETATION, APPLICATION, IMPLEMENTATION), ALLOWING THEM TO START AT THEIR CURRENT SKILL LEVEL AND DIVE INTO THE MEAT OF THE WORD OF GOD.

WHETHER YOU ARE A CHAPLAIN LOOKING FOR RESOURCES FOR YOUR UNIT, A CHURCH WITH ACTIVE DUTY MEMBERS OR A SOLDIER, SAILOR, AIRMAN OR MARINE THAT NEEDS A FIELD-READY DEVOTIONAL GUIDE, MOTD FITS THE BILL. THE YEAR IS BROKEN DOWN INTO 12 ONE-MONTH SECTIONS WITH A USER GUIDE THAT INTRODUCES THE "WHY" AND "HOW" OF INDUCTIVE BIBLE STUDY.

FOLLOW AND LIKE MILITARY DEVOS FOR DAILY DEVO THOUGHTS:

 @MILITARYDEVOS

FACEBOOK.COM/MILITARYDEVOS

MILITARYDEVOTIONAL.COM

 PILGRIMAGE EDUCATIONAL RESOURCES
1362 FORDS POND RD
CLARKS SUMMIT, PA 18411

Made in the USA
Middletown, DE
02 September 2024

60255288R00015